THE UNSPOKEN SYMPHONY

poems

THE UNSPOKEN SYMPHONY

poems

BOLUTIFE OLUWADELE

Winepress
by NOIRLEDGE

ISBN: 978-978-61043-6-2

Published in Nigeria by Winepress Publishing
In association with The Village Boy Academy
Website: www.thevillageboi.com | Email: author@thevillageboi.com

Scan the QR code below to access the author's Amazon page:

Winepress Publishing
Suite 223, Ogun-Oshun River Basin Development Authority,
Off Oni Memorial Children's Hospital, Ring-Road, Ibadan
Telephone: +234 809 816 4359 | +234 909 666 4359
Email: hello@noirledge.com | Website: www.noirledge.com
Socials: www.linktr.ee/noirledge

Winepress Publishing is an imprint of Noirledge Limited. For information regarding discounts on bulk purchases and special editions of our titles, please contact our Sales Department via hello@noirledge.com or +234 809 8164 359.

Cover Design: Dhee Sylvester
Book Design: Servio Gbadamosi
Typesetting: Kayode Sanni
Printed and bound in Nigeria by Noirledge Limited

Dedication

This collection is dedicated to the glory of God, who continually inspires me. Additionally, I would like to thank my readers, whose feedback continues to motivate me to write.

Acknowledgements

I am greatly indebted to so many people on my writing journey.

However, it becomes so tasking to remember all those "Angels' who have stood solidly with me.

To Mr. & Mrs Ayelokun, whose unwavering support is beyond description. Mrs. Bose Baggot's support is nearly impossible to quantify. All my colleagues at ICAN Canada and the District Society (ICDS) are the real MVPs.

At the home base are Adewale Adedeji, Damilola Akintobi, Mr. and Mrs. Toluwaleyi, Michael Olaogun, Kunle Bamidele, and many more; I am indeed grateful.

The Oluwadeles whose time I always 'steal' to get all these together, your support is not taken for granted.

To all my friends, too numerous to mention, especially Mr. & Mrs. Adeola and Richard Sotande, I cannot thank you enough.

My apologies for the prominent names that are missing again. God bless you all for all your kind support.

Preface

Each soul is its own chorus, its own musical mix of experiences, ideas, visions and whispers that mould the fabric of our being. We might share the music with others, but so much goes unexpressed, concealed in the silence of our hearts and minds. *The Unspoken Symphony* is a collection that hopes to unleash these silenced melodies, to give us a glimpse into human introspection where words fail us yet are alive in the silence between words.

This collection is borne of self-reflection and compassion, of an understanding that our silent narratives are as powerful and beautiful as the ones we tell. Here, I have attempted to encapsulate some of life's quieter truths, the whispered insight, the whispered chords that sing us through, and the contrasts that give us the idea of love, loss, resilience and belonging.

Each composition reminds us to slow down and hear the song in our lives. You will read about friendship, intuition, the silent power of loneliness, and the ghosts of our past echoing in our present. These are not treated as solutions but rather as questions for you to play with in your own head as you read.

While you're reading *The Unspoken Symphony*, I hope you can find yourself in the mirror with these words and know that the unspoken elements of your story are beautiful and right. I hope you find these pages as a kind of gentle guide, connecting you to your quiet symphony in yourself and perhaps moving you to perform your own silent symphony for the world.

Introduction

Life moves on the delicate sand between speech and silence, of speaking and non-speaking. Our lips often paint our faces, but what's unsaid – the inner musings, the closeness of feelings, the dream in the lonely house – is what makes us who we are. *The Unspoken Symphony* is a look into this world of unspoken reality, a musical tour through the things that hold us together as humans, even when we are at our most private.

This collection is organized into themes, each focused on the diverse aspects of our inner lives. All chapters are curated around the universal experiences we encounter at the core of our existence: from the discussions of *Love and Connection* to the reflections of *Self-Discovery and Intuition*, the conflict of *Joy and Sorrow* to the awakenings of *Silence and Solitude*. In this collection, you will find poems that reflect the raw beauty of a smile, the quiet heroism of strength, and the intricate wonder of non-verbal friendships.

So, too, does *The Unspoken Symphony* embrace the juxtaposition of the human condition. Happiness and sadness in Joy and Sorrow are often held together in our bodies, complementing each other. In The Power of Intuition, we discover how our inner voice and intuitions will carry us through life's dark lands to provide guidance when reason is not. And, in The Worthiness of Friendship, we think about how strong a friend can be and what kind of promise, of undeniable bonds, friendship makes.

This volume is more than a collection of musings; it is an invitation to listen to your inner music and hear the songs that shape your own life. Every poem and line is meant to function as a mirror of the poet's life but also of the reader's, an arena of contemplation, perhaps healing. It is a phrase to be heard, sung with the sound of it slowly, that shakes you as you move through your own process.

While you read, I hope you'll take some time to sit in the space between words, hear those small voices coming to you silently, and experience the feeling of being among us on this page. *The Unspoken Symphony* is an adolescent hymn to the silence, an adolescent homage to the faint harmony that ties us together. May these thoughts become your own musical composition, helping you to sing with and through the pauses of your own journey.

Contents

poems

The Power of Agreement [1]

Like the legendary Magi
That bestrode the landscape
In homage visitation
To the newly born Messiah
These Three in Unison
Demanded another baby boy
In the most emphatic gesticulations
From the bewildered parents.

Far from the contemplation
Of hibernation in the oza ruum
But with mouths agape
At such audacity of convictions
From children in the minority years
Who are not deterred by their demand
Even if they did not know how
That would come to be.

Then the deed was done
Watched as it developed
Anti-natal visitations religiously observed
In the days when scanning was an exception
Waiting for who will be brought forth
With fingers crossed
But the children refusing
To be convinced otherwise

____

[1] Adapted from the true story of a wise man, Ezenwa Echefu.

When the final day arrived
With the hubby standing akimbo
Pacing up and down the labour room
The convinced Magi
Were busy designing placard
With the ubiquitous words written
"Welcome home, baby Samuel."
Because we asked him of the Lord.

True to their convictions
It turned out that a baby boy
Was added to the family
To give them a balanced team
Of equal numbers of genders
Just because the initial Three
The Magi of the Lord
Were unshaken in their convictions
That is the power of agreement.

The Blurry Tunnel Vision

Delicately etching on the precipice
With the demeanour of Habakkuk
Hoping for clarity of becoming morrow
Yet looking like a lost soldier in mammy market.

Seeing a tiny thread of hope
Grabbing with both hands for grips,
Turned out to be broken beyond repairs
A hope dashed before it even starts.

An array of gladiators
In disbanded trolley of governance
Whipping up the ecstasy of delightfulness
Only to be more of an expended cannon.

2023 is a date beholding
Assuaging the frailty of extended wantonness
From a well-crafted plummet
Of sacrificial leadership.

This gazing nonetheless,
Into the crystal ball of hope,
Is revealing heart wrenchcs,
Of blurry tunnel vision.

Father's Day 2022

The avalanche of felicitations
The poignancy of the wordings
Eliciting euphoric gyration
From a profoundly appreciative soul
To a Supreme Creator
For Divine Blessings, unencumbered
And in supplication for struggling fathers
For a new season of abundant harvesting
From the hidden teary sowings.
Happy Father's Day to all.

The Survivalist

the joy of victory
the affiliated ownerships of success
few meters away
from the orphanage of failures
survived the "Pándòrò"
out of its stormy enclave

The Worthiness of Friendship

Life is hounded with accidents
　　　Some circumstantial
　　　　　Many in fleeting moments
　　　　　　　Yet many others leave incurable scars

Then there is a friendship greater than the blood bonds
　　　Where vulnerability becomes an haven
　　　　　Friendship that is beyond transactional
　　　　　　　Friendship that is compassionately caring.

Thank you for the gift of friendship!

Smiles!

I smile
Yes, I do
When I smile
Where I smile
How I smile
Moments make me smile
Then your smile
Make me smile the more.

The Corruption We Do Not Want to Fight

The farmer had cleared the land, sowed his seeds, and fed his flock
The rains fell in due season
The farm machinery was in full throttle

Then the locusts came
And ate all the farm
The quelea birds came too
And completed the pestilence

We woke up and saw the polis tricked by politicians
who fixed a high price to buy the forms to fill and contest to rule us
Eyes and hearts fixed on the harvest from our common barn

Unlike the farmer who weeds his farm and tends his flock and fights
any pest and disease threatening his farm and flock

Our politicians are the pests in our pestilence
Hands dripping with oil
Which they lick and laugh
And mock us daily

No doubt any longer
That this is the corruption
We never wanted to fight
From the beginning of time.

When it is Beyond Your Reach!

I could recollect the name of the goalkeeper vividly
He was called Jawando from one of the neighbouring schools
Then there was this our school Striker
His name refused to resonate again
He had come to retake the WASSCE
A powerful shooter who uses both legs.

We were awarded a penalty kick
Not three corners make one goal
It was a deserving penalty
The striker went a few meters backing the goalkeeper
Came back, mesmerizing the keeper
The keeper was not sure with which leg he would shoot.

Boom! He fired the shot
Jawando dodged it!
What?
Is this not Jawando?
Mythically compared with Okala
The man with the mystery magnetic gloves.

As a 'certified' Aproko
I went to eavesdrop at the camp of the opponents
What will they tell or ask Jawando?
True to my expectations, he was asked
Ogbeni (Mr.), why did you not even attempt the shot?
You dodged it and allowed them to win.

He retorted sharply to the accusation.
Wọ à yọ mú rú rẹ?
Translated, "can you catch that kind."
I wanted to laugh out loud
But I quickly ran to a safe corner
Where I released my hysterical laughter.

Sometimes we face the challenges
Of meeting up expectations
And facing the reality of the situations
Jawando was more realistic
Because the striker's shot was deadly
He avoided becoming a 'victim.'

As I attempted to take a walk yesterday,
My boy warned me about the weather outside.
I assured him that I would turn back if it became tougher
But I made it for a few kilometres
The street was unusually scanty
I wondered why people did not come to play

It was during the solitude of walking
That I remembered the Jawando episode
And saw a great lesson in what he did
He calculated his chances of parrying the ball
However, concluded there was no point.
He could not possibly save his 'world.'

When it is beyond your reach
Evaluate and retreat
We live to fight another day

There will still be many days ahead
So, take it easy on yourself
Some days we win, other days we lose
Do not overstretch when it is beyond your limit
There, is the risk of irreparably breaking.

Do you agree with me?
You do not have to
But always evaluate
Attempt if you can.
Happy boxing day!
Do not box oversize persons, please!

Seeking True Love

It is sometimes ridiculed
Other times highly elevated
Then we try to personalize it
Just because we all seek
For true love.

The Good Neighbour: Are You One?

Beyond space and time
Deeper than friendship
Angels watching over each other
That is what good neighbours do.

The aura of safety
A shoulder to lean on
Giving succour to the weary
Is the joy of a good neighbour.

Are you a good neighbour?
Or a mere space sharer?
You can still step up
And become a good neighbour.

The Convergence

Once upon a convergence
The realignment occurs
Of fragmented notions
Crystallizing into tangible
Strategies for enactment
Paving unambiguous ways
Towards the fated
Amazonian Eldorado.

Nothing is Absolute!

A bright sunny day in winter
Alluring walking around, folks
Speaking clearly to the soul
No condition is permanent.

Nothing seems absolute
Be it right or wrong
Validity of perspectives
Trumping absoluteness.

The Power of Intuition

It drops like a UFO
Right in the recesses
Of our inner being
Making no sense at first

Some novel thoughts
Pervading the imagination
With nothing concrete
To substantiate its reality

Quite often neglected
Convincing power alienated
Like a parasitic invasion
Of personal solitude

Then like a bang
Its life occurrence
Jostled us back into reality
I had this feeling all along

Intuition is powerful
Guiding through the rough patches
If only we are circumspect
And listen more to our intuition

The Missing Object

I have gripped the cutlass
To search for the missing cutlass in the grass
The phone torchlight
To look for the misplaced phone
The writer's pen fully inked
For the missing pen
The writer cannot write
Because the pen he holds
Is meant to find the pen
In the parody of life

A Note on Intuition

intuition falls like a rock
and you scamper to
do its bidding, or it erupts like a volcano
from a molten sense
inside your being
destroying your sensibilities

leaving a damp ash,
this fiery fire
comes with new thought
like a tendril of a flower

a new scene and sense
fills your solitude
multitudes gather in the invasion
Of your privacy

and you rise
to eject them by describing
their intrusion, and they leave you

with a new insight
like an unexpected promise, kept
intuition is a visitation
a leading to new lights

if you receive the intrusion
and the voice or nudge
it urges you to adopt

you get new insights

from your guts
and a sense of knowing
as if you have already known
the reality that had existed
before you brought it to being

What If?

It is safer in the dark
And dangerous on noonday
Joyful in hunger
But sadness in opulence

The best produces the worst
And the despised the best
One good head
Is better than ten others

The healthy dies
And the sickly lives on
The rich go bankrupt
And the poor, financially stable

No one knows
What might always be
Hence, we should remember
What if it is otherwise.

The Mindset

In the fluidity of time
Holding breath
As if the clock
Ticks differently
Faster when engaging
And slower when lazing about
Just only in the mind.

Spring of Life

Buried in snow
With near hopelessness
Then the sun melted away
And the soil opens its bowels
Receiving new seeds
While the dead scrubs revived
And the fuzzy turns green
Giving food to the eaters
Welcome to the new season
The Spring of Life.

The Cloudy Sky

Gaze up
And behold a cloudy sky
Bringing into remembrance
When it was once void
And the beauties of the unknown
And a questioning yearning

Like a farmer gauging
The planting season
Like the voyager
Entrapped in a maze
Confused about the road
To take

Then jostled suddenly
As in fever-induced
Hallucinations
But brought back to life
And echoing the old hymn
Showers of blessings.

Then the outpouring
Not seasonal only
But continuously restoring
The famished soul
To its factory setting
And cloudiness yields
Grounds to new refreshing

The cloudy sky
What a harbinger!
Unlocking trapped greatness
But now, in torrents
Restoration unhindered
Breathing a new lease
Of life in unobtrusive flow

The Golden Key

With a doubtful mind
Hidden like the Ostriches
In their bunkers
Yet peeping out
In the similute of a Stargazer.

Afterwards
Being called unto the podium
Pronounced the confirmation
Of a melting heart
By the Prince Charming.

In a worthwhile voyage
Transcending uneven terrains
Yet building strong affinities
Finally leading to
An affirmation
Of love undiluted

Such is the golden key
Unlocking the unyielding hearts
Transmitting to a blossom
Watered Gardens
Of undiluted affections
Fruitfully blessed
At the time of life.

Of Double Serving Single

It takes two eyes to see
And two ears to hear
What one mouth speaks

Two for one
One for two
Two givers and
One receiver
In divine arrangement
Is this uncanny mystery
Of being
Discernable
Only by the wise

Greater knowledge
Serving deeper wisdom
But wisdom
Is greater
Than knowledge

Many steps
Leading to one end
Many efforts
In the hands of one destiny

Life rolls
And gravitates to one goal
Like many followers
Surrounding the leader
For one purpose.

The Line in Between

There is the point
Where the oscillation
Of the opposite
Poles of nature
Are first drawn

But they are blurred
And you pick
Your way from
One extremity
To the other
In your journey in life

Sanity and insanity
Wisdom and folly
Prosperity and poverty
Good and evil
Joy and sorrow
Life and death
Laughter and Wailing
Love and Hate

And so, you turn
Making and dropping
From one point
To the other
Dangling in between
The poles.

The Dilemma

There is a blurry line in between
The oscillation of thoughts,
And it creates an unspoken dilemma.

The line in between lingers
And dailies like a pendulum,
From one extreme to the other.

Action waits the struggle
To choose any of the extremes.

Moderation stands and tinkers
On a precipice, daring consequences.

Ignorance fuels the need for the extreme
Of a desperate action.

Consciousness, always the gatekeeper, pulls
In the direction of caution.

Wisdom intervenes with fresh insight
Using vigilance as guide.

And so, the road to decision
Continues, unwittingly trapped
In an infinite loop of dilemma.

The 'I Can' in the ICAN

Yes, I can
The dexterity of purpose
Diligence and commitment
Driven by passion
As the gatekeeper
Of the commonwealth

The I in the ICAN
Orchestrated by the search
To balance
The debit and credit
Constantly interfacing
To create stability

The I in the ICAN
With tentacles
Spread across all divides
A governance champion
Dressed in modesty
And sober in talk

The I in the ICAN
'Tis time to rise
And take charge
And navigate the uncharted
As the harbinger
In the disruptive space
Of technology
The I in the ICAN

The power of resilience
Undaunted by obstacles
Energized to make a difference
The leading voice
In the chambers of decision-makers

The I in the ICAN
Noble and full of integrity
Candid and true
Bound by Trust
Far above mediocrity
For service delivery

Who Are You?

Who are you?
I am XYZ
What is your name?
My name is XYZ.

Then, who are you?
I just told you my name
Your name only identifies you
But that is who I am.

No! Still, who are you?
I am getting confused
Why are you confused?
Is my name not who am I?

What are your values?
Your convictions
The point on which you stand, sealed,
The essence of your being.

What do you represent?
Your buy in process
Your dispositions to issues
How do you treat others?

Again, who are you?
All these make me who I am?
Yes, they do
How, then, do I answer the question?

Does the question sound simple?
Is it not that undeniable
Perhaps it is an easy tease
What is complicated with the question?

Yes, it may seem simple
Is it not?
The simple questions are the most difficult to answer
Why is it so?

We thought they were a walkover
And answer them offhandedly
Without chewing them in bits of memory
And we are thrown off balance

Look at the mirror of yourself
And take a deep breath
Straightway gaze into your inner being
And ask yourself
Who really am I?

Of Time and Season II

It is no longer
Strange to any observer
That time and season
Abounds

Time to start
And time to end
In between the poles
Are issues accountable

It may be great,
Or not so great
Perhaps something in between
The legs of the period

It may start with
Many expectations
Unbridled excitement
In a confusing cobweb

In the passing moment
Reality sets in
As water finds its level
Something has to give

In some instances
The starting is sudden
As much as the ending
In a vicious cycle kind of

Do not get too enmeshed
In the infinity loops
And become unduly settled
In a passing phase

Learn to say goodbye
To the old season
And usher in with hope
The newly baked season

No matter the outcome
Of the season past
It offers its lessons
If we do well to observe

Oh, that the new season
Is worth more than the last
No matter how great
The last season was.

The Symphony of Self-Knowledge

In a world full of knowledge
Coached by the social media
Yet lost in its cacophony
Is knowledge of self.

From the teenage years
Sandwiched in peer pressures
To be shared as morsels
In the life for many.

Many a people
Fluff in borrowed wings
Of perceived best practices
Even if unpalatable to them

But the few
That unearth self-knowledge
Are transformed by
The symphony of self-discovery.

The Mirage

It is everyone's albatross
Even the wisest can be dumb
And struck by the power of illusion
And call it vanity

Then reality dawns
In a wavering manner
That confuses more
Than it convinces

The labyrinth of its
Falsehood
Always appearing truthful
Remains in its precincts

Though we always have a choice
To demystify its lie
Or be caught unawares
In its ubiquitous traps

Similitude of a faded mirror
Whose images become
Illusory afterward
Is a mirage to the undiscerning
It may present itself

As tales too tall
And hills too steep to climb
And Valleys too deep to descend

Its potent antidote
Lies in the curious mindset
Of the undeterred warrior
Breaking the artificial barrier
And setting self free.

The Burden of Life

It comes in varied
Shapes and sizes
At different times
In diverse ways

The duration varies
And the weight is unequal
With unpredictable turn
For everyone

Scarcely is anyone immune
From its pangs
Though it is not always welcome
It shows up its head

While some bear it alone
Others shift it
Yet some curtail it
It drowns so many

No point denying it
It produces no superman
Its denial often prolongs
The inescapable torments

When you are not bearing
Yours for the moment
Despise not those pressed
By its heavy weight

They are not always meant
To last for ever
But can resurface
When not properly borne

No one wishes for it
Notwithstanding it shows up
It is good sense
To bear it with dignity

Pay Attention, Please!

Whenever you are trapped
In the slick web of the daily
hustle and bustle
Pay attention.

On the precipice
Of a fallen cliff
With the deep blue ocean below
Please pay attention.

In the valley of decision
Blurry with perspectives
About the issue on the table
Remember to pay attention.

On top of the mountain
In the exhilarating ecstasy
Of a dream fulfilled
Do not forget to pay attention.

In the womb of
The bright morning,
Where the alluring sunshine bristles
Do pay attention.

When in public embrace
Of the unfriendly friend,
Foes pretending to be friends,
Be sure to pay attention.

Whenever served hot,
The ala carte of disappointment
From unexpected quarters,
It is necessary to pay attention.

In all the journey
Traversing life in its finitude
No matter the outcome
Just pay attention.

Of the Silly Dove

A silly dove
You are
A silly dove
You will be

If you don't quit
Silliness and understand
The duality
Of our existence

You have to know
That some days are filled
With evil tidings
And others with glad tidings

Or you will slip
And slump like Samson
Who moonlighted with succulence
And lost his destiny.

Chaffing Justice

Pench up the sky
Seated the wielders of Damocles
Their feckle demeanour
Dish out injustice
Fooling none but themselves

Better than the judged
So, their poor judgement feels
Only in their imagination
Their gavel seals the fate of hapless litigants
Who, for want of a banal court
Carry chaff for wheat of justice
Endure the charade and facade of justice.

How dare you? Their echo faints
In the supposedly hallowed chambers of equity
Where truth tiptoes
When wigs and glasses are adjusted
To utter yet another dissembles

Their Judgemental 'gospel'
Beguiling the ignorant
And the unthinking stooges
Foolishly propagating same

Until the veil is ripped
By the boisterous human entanglement
Revealing the Janus dispensers of law
Peddling justice for favour, protection, or cash

Hypocritical judges they exemplify

Did the harbingers
And co-conspirators
 Realize that they are
Mere Judgemental 'gospellers'

Quit your elevated falsehood
Accept the reality
Of human fallibility
That exempts no one.

What do you even gain?
In the campaign of calumny
Against your fellow voyagers
In the short journey of life!

The Deceitful Shadow

I know we were buddies
Like Siamese twins
Never to be separated
From one another

But you brought the buts
When you started walking
In the opposite direction
Away from my path

When I turned left
I saw you taking a detour
To the right side
Then I switched lane
To the right
But you switched to the left

We were walking together
Under the eyes of the sun
Savouring the shining sunlight
Which gave way to the dusk
Then I lost sight of you
In the dim of the half-moon.

How can you not be
Consistent with me
As a companion
Through all patches

Why will you disappear
Into the dark alley of an unlit night
But beckon to me
With a princely gait
At sunrise

Then, following my protest
Of your inconsistent companionship
You confidently affirm that
You have always been with me

How deceitful can that be
When I search for you
In the dead of the night
And no one shows up

When I yearn to speak with someone
Why are you not responding to
My inner thoughts
If indeed you are always here

My shadow
All time company
Playing recluse with me
At the most critical time

A deceitful shadow
Who goes dumb and deaf
When attention is most needed

Oh, the still small voice
That echoes the unspoken lines
Is a stronger companion
Than the ubiquitous shadow!

Voice of Silence

You kept mute
Not minding the anger
Of hateful people
Parroting all around you
With loud voices

Though they threaten
Speak up now
Or else, we deal with you
Bold red, popping eyes
Hiding their deep fears
Of insecurity and unsafety

Yet, you keep your cool
Not shifting your gaze
From their jittery mien
Presented as boldfaces
To determine your best option

What is wrong with you?
They echo
Confused as they come
At the audacity of your silence

In hush whispers
They confer with each other
Bereft, of how else
To pull you out
Of this dignified silence

Oh, powerful silence!
Deadly as the graveyard
Tucked in between.
Isolated terrestrial abode
Of some esoteric beings.

The voice of silence is powerful
Beyond the comprehension
Of the glass hearted
Masquerading as supermen
If you do not cringe

Only the wise
With a spirit that discerns
Can truly hear
The uncommon echo
Of calculated silence
For it speaks louder
Than the roaring lion
Whose next meal is unsure
The voice of silence is powerful.

Double-Tongued Allies

Almost the entire landscape
Is filled with double-faced
And double-tongued masquerades
Garbed as friends

The envious Cain
Slaughtering the Righteous Abel
And the greedy Lot
Short-changing Uncle Abe

Then, the manipulative Jacob
With the food-starved Esau
In the tasty porridge
Entanglement of a long throat

A loud hosanna at noon
Followed closely afterward
In an unabated frenzy
Crucify him above criminals

Green with envy
Denying the commanded
Neighbourly Agape love
For harmonious existence

So are the double-tongued
And usually double-faced parading as allies
Entrapping the gullible and innocent folks
With their shark teeth

The Kenery once sang
In his sonorous voice of a legend
Called Orlando Owoh
Of the lost species

Called friends and relations
Even good neighbours
All gone way too far
Into irretrievable extinction

Trust them not
Neither depend nor rely on them
Keep them at best a decent distance
As acquittances for socialization

The Unhelpful Helper

Rudely interrupted
On a long-distance call
With the unknown address
To one with half engagement.

Hey, bros can you help?
Address flipped off the phone
To get the direction
Getting there on time.

Oh, that?
I guess your best bet
Is the Google Map
To chaperon you safely.

How on earth!
Would you disrupt
A flowing conversation
Rather than self-help.

It turned out
That the projected helper
Cannot do anything
Since concentration was limited.
Have you been in such situation?
When you ignorantly approach
A total stranger
Hoping to be helped?

What a waste
When the opposite happens
To be the result
Of an unhelpful helper.

The Weather Man

not the Meteorologist
forecasting the weather
helping us to plan ahead
and dress up for the day

'tis the oscillating being
who is neither cold nor hot
yet far away from in between
confusing all who
trust in them
perpetually astride on the fence

usually up to no good
betrayal a sport
backstabbing a delight
to the warped mind
of unconscienced being
unstable as the Chinook weather.

Unconventional Being

An unconventional person
Never fits into the stereotype
Never meant to be
Walking alone
In the dark alley of the mind
Hears only own voice
Moving against the tide
But with purpose
Only inwardly driven
May be celebrated afterwards
When he arrives at the destined end

Knowing Yourself

Who are you?
In the minds of others
Among your kitchen cabinet
Within your inner recess

Can you answer this
All by yourself
With no outside influence
Or you need external validation?

You are who you are
Internalize and own it
And find the equilibrium
Where it is possible

Misalignments Unresolved

Woke up yet again
With conflicting thoughts
On how to go on
Find a path from this crossroads

My mind directs leftward
And the heart rightward
Instincts echoing hold on
External forces beckon a return

In these cacophonies
Amidst decibels of voice
Misalignments rise
And unresolved actions lie

Poetic Prophecy

Outsource your understanding
Despising knowledge
Is greatly unwise
And a risky flight

Thanksgiving in Canada

Golden leaves and crisp, cool air,
Families gather, love to share.
Tables laden with autumn's best,
Gratitude in every guest.

Pumpkin pies and turkey roast,
Memories made, we cherish most.
Laughter, stories, joy, and cheer,
Thanksgiving time, our hearts sincere.

Finding Yourself

Trapped in the mire
Hanging in between shrubs
Encircled among thorns
Do what you have to do
But make sure
You find yourself
The real you
And run with that

The Family Dynamics

Like all things evolving
Once closely knitted
As gatherers of food
For subsistence and coexistence

In the community building
Looking out for each other
With care and love
Devoid of hate and division

Then the atoms of disintegration
Of once cherished affinity
Broke into semi nuclear abode
Of close relatives and greed

Came with the fangs of economic pangs
Coupled with the rat race
Of uneasy survival
Eating into ultra-nuclear settings.

Our sense of community was eaten
The thread of unity and ties, torn
Leaving us howling with selfishness
Our pride of Ubuntu destroyed

Grateful Heart

To all who gave their glow and joy,
Thank you so much for your love,
Your whims filled me with light and sweetness,
And my heart, with a smile.

With each message, phone call, and prayer,
You made me realize that you really care,
Thanks for every one of the words,
I thank you all from my heart.

Winter's Early Whisper

Outside, a cold wind calls in Calgary's avenues.
A silence of cold spells.
Even before the leaves could drop, there was nothing to do.
Winter arrived, cloaking all.

The Bow River's chorus fades silent and placid.
Its reflective surface cools.
Mountains don snowy crowns overnight,
A flamboyant sign of the winter's power.

Clouds descend, a silvery shroud,
Mountains and blanketed houses.
Breath appears clear against cool morning air.
A frozen kiss that still hangs there.

The evergreens, proud sentinels, stand,
Their boughs stoked with Mother Nature.
While the city streets sparkle under moon's light,
Winter's early darkness has its magic spell.

Children cheer as snowflakes fly,
Calgary sees its first snowmen.
But whispers tell of long nights ahead, and the dark is coming.
Of snowy highways and well-stocked fireplaces.

O Calgary, how you charm and punish,
Early winters are unmissable.
And we find strength in you, that we endure.
And beauty in cold is always pure.

More Than Socks and Ties

Today, we stop, sigh, and look.
To treat men with respect.
Fathers, brothers, friends, and peers,
Dream-builders through blood and tears.

And yet, there's a curious trend we can't get away from.
It was the same story, over and over.
How could their offerings be so simple, so plain?
Tie, socks, boxers—again and again.

Is it the blind world?
The depth of men's complexity?
Their hearts, their heads, their non-verbal struggle.
Their might, day, and night?

And beyond the jobs they're tasked with.
They imagine, they expect, they snicker, they hope.
A gift needs to be a reflection of itself.
Not a flag to be proud of.

So let us give priority to the more significant, what is more significant?
Thank you, a relationship that's built into us.
Time to pass, a warm greeting,
A sign that they're special.

Men are not entitled to tie dyed patterns.
Or socks in unfamiliar colours.
Give them respect, give them affection, give them respect.
Celebrate their worth enough.

For all the men who have defended themselves, I salute you.
Whose silent courage does astound,
Let's defy the grain and change the game, eh?
Honour every man as a companion.

Walking on the Snow

Deep snow falls beneath my feet.
A world slumbering in silence.
Pathways piled with winter's might,
Yet here I walk, defying the white.

Each footfall is slow, sharp, hard, smooth.
The murmured crunch when the air is frigid.
The ice bites, the wind itches, the twilight fades.
But a flame scorches king in my heart.

For ice breath tests in nature, keep a long finger on the pulse button.
Its elegance severs with whispered murder.
Yet humans rise, undaunted, strong,
We make our way along icy trails.

The snow, its canvas empty and wide.
Record my journey, present and past.
Each footstep embodies outspoken rebellion, defiance.
A hushed anthem to our resilience.

The ice might shove, the storm might howl.
Yet passion drives us evermore.
We do not walk simply to be somewhere, though.
But to face the obstacle.

So, I push through the winter's labyrinth, and it swells away.
Over icy bridges and clouded fog.
For life, for expanding dreams,
I feel happy, tromping the snow.

Change if You Must

Change, if you will, for the bendable heart.
Knows the truth when it comes time to rest.
Repentance calls, a sacred plea,
To loosen the bonds and liberate the spirit.

Be the change, growth draws you to
New perspectives, new grounds to tread.
Like the seed that cracks to reach the sky.
We shift to free, we shift to ascend.

Turn around, for opportunity awaits.
In other realms, beyond the old gates.
If you want to meet the self you never knew, then create one for
yourself.
Step out, sweeten the deal.

Change if you must, for errors are blaring, mistaken.
Echoes of lessons, in proud bearings
Right the wrongs, bring back the past,
And steer where truths stand firm.

Move if you need to, to achieve your goal.
To fill your heart with the fire of purpose.
Unshackle the anxiety that keeps you trapped.
And dared to act on its own accord

Turn if you must, for mercy drops
You leave the wounded place.
The scars may linger but the hope will bloom.

And quiet where the blood had been shed.

Change if you need to, for life is a stream,
Ever flowing, shaping dreams.
Ride the wave, be firm, follow your heart.
New worlds are bound to unfold

Do not fear the change, the untrod
Make a turn if you must, let the light shine
To change is not to perish,
But to wake, and to choose.

Unheard Whispers of an Author

Behind the words, a story untold,
An author's heart, both brave and bold.
Misconceptions swirl, like ink on the page,
But beyond the surface, lies the quiet sage.

Not for riches, nor for gold,
But for the stories that must be told.
In every line, in every rhyme,
An author's journey, beyond time.

In the silence of the night, where thoughts run deep,
A writer's soul finds solace, dreams they keep.
For every word, a piece of heart they give,
In every book, their essence lives.

People see the cover, but not the strain,
The silent struggles, the unseen pain.
Yet, through each hurdle, they rise and persist,
For within their veins, stories twist.
It's not the wealth that defines their art,
But the passion burning in their heart.
Every page turned, every tale spun,
Is a battle fought, and sometimes won.

So, let them think of pockets deep,
For it's the words that secrets keep.
An author's wealth is not in coin or gold,
But in the stories that forever unfold.

Each dawn brings a new tale to weave,
A canvas blank, on which dreams conceive.
Through highs and lows, through dark and light,
The author's pen continues its flight.
Their ink is blood, their script, a vein,
Pouring life into pages, joy, and pain.
For every reader, a piece of soul,
A glimpse into the heart, whole.

They craft worlds, where minds can wander,
A tapestry of thought, inviting ponder.
So, let the myths and whispers spread,
For an author's legacy is in the words they've written.

Behind the scenes, where few may peer,
Lies the heart of the writer, sincere.
Not for acclaim, nor fleeting fame,
But for the love of the story, untamed.

OTHER BOOKS BY BOLUTIFE OLUWADELE, PhD

MY QUEST FOR NIGERIA'S REBIRTH

My Quest for Nigeria's Rebirth explores Nigeria's unique social challenges, aiming to spark profound contemplation and ignite a collective drive for positive change. Within the pages of this book, readers will explore the intricate web of socio-political issues that have long hindered progress while offering a rallying cry to harness our nation's abundant human and material resources for the betterment of all.

This thought-provoking narrative charts a course toward a brighter future, uniting us in the pursuit of a common good that uplifts the lives of everyday Nigerians.

BUSINESS STRATEGY MANUAL

Business Strategy Manual is an engaging compilation of essential business tips based on the author's years of practice and experience. It is a book specifically designed for small and medium-sized enterprises (SMEs) and other businesses seeking to optimize their performance and make informed decisions. With practical examples and case studies, the book aims to equip business owners with the knowledge the skills necessary to harness the power of data and transform it into actionable business strategies. From identifying market trends to evaluating customer behaviour, *Business Strategy Manual* is a valuable resource for SMEs looking to stay competitive in today's data-driven business landscape.

ODDITY OF IMPUNITY

Oddity of Impunity serves us with freshness and unhindered expressiveness, salted with the self-mastery of an adept satirist. With playful sternness, the poet writes about issues that plague us daily—democratisation, corruption, exploitation, and Pan-Africanism; asking us to take action, so we can truly play while we work.

THOUGHTS OF A VILLAGE BOY

In contemplating the course of history, it becomes evident that the narratives of tomorrow are intricately shaped by the chronicles of today. *Thoughts of a Village Boy* unveils a profound exploration of authentic issues, subtly interwoven with contemporary events, all set within the heart of the most populous nation on the African continent. The book stands as a significant contribution to the existing tapestry of literature dedicated to the modern history of Nigeria. It delves into a spectrum of vital themes deeply entrenched in the nation's fabric, which, though universal in nature, are uniquely addressed, offering readers an enlightening journey back to the very roots of our collective history.

BUDGETING MADE SIMPLE

Many business owners struggle with budgeting. In fact, it scares many of them. In this simple-to-read book, we have broken down the process in simple language for easy comprehension. Budgeting is an essential tool for running any successful business, and, therefore, should not be neglected by all means.

Read this book and apply all the principles narrated therein, and you will be on your way to running a successful and sustainable business.

SUSTAINABLE CASH FLOW

This book is written as a guide or a compass for small business owners to easily navigate through the murky waters of cash flow management. As we know that sustainability in business is heavily depended on successful cashflows, therefore, adequate knowledge of how it works will help a lot.

BACK TO THE FUTURE

Back to the Future: A Collection of Dialogical Poems in Pidgin uses wit, satire, and allegory to spotlight pressing socio-economic and political issues in contemporary society. Written in accessible Nigerian Pidgin, these 25 engaging poems blend humor with hard truths, using a dialogical style to provoke thought and inspire change. Both lively and sobering, this collection speaks to readers across social divides with clarity, urgency, and cultural authenticity.

SACRED CROSSROADS

Sacred Crossroads: Balancing Culture, Faith, and Modern Life offers a thoughtful guide to navigating the tensions between tradition and modernity. Across 19 chapters, it explores how timeless values and cultural identity can coexist with today's fast-paced world. With practical insights on faith, resilience, and purpose, this book empowers readers to live authentically and spiritually grounded lives in an ever-changing society.

Bolutife Oluwadele, a Canada-based versatile Chartered Accountant, holds a PhD and Master of Public Administration (with Distinction) in Public Policy and Administration from Walden University, USA, as well as a Master of Science degree in Corporate Govern-ance from Leeds University, England.

Bolutife is a renowned Certified Fraud Examiner, cerebral Public Policy Scholar accomplished Trainer, and Business/General Management Consultant.

A very prolific and satiric author, he has published bestsellers such as "Thoughts of a Village Boy," "My Quest for Nigeria's Rebirth," "Business Strategy Manual," and "Oddity of Impunity," among others. He attended Ayetoro/Iloro High School (AIHS), Ekiti State, and the Federal College of Education, Katsina, Nigeria where he studied History/CRS before transiting to become a certified professional accountant.

Bolutife, a diligent, intelligent, and resilient multi-disciplinary professional, was once honored with an award for Technical Concept Development for the Canada International Accountants' Conference of the Institute of Chartered Accountants of Nigeria (ICAN). He was also honored with the book "Counting Green" by Samuel Ogabidu, a poet, to mark his Diamond Jubilee.